Spring FREEZE

By: Sarah Muehlbauer

WATERHORSE PRESS

Copyright © October 10, 2015

All rights reserved. No part of this book may be used or reproduced by any means, graphic, electronic, or mechanical, including photocopying, recording, taping or by any information storage retrieval system without the written permission of the publisher except in the case of brief quotations embodied in critical articles and reviews. Views expressed in this work are solely those of the author and do not necessarily reflect the views of the publisher, and the publisher hereby disclaims any responsibility for them.

First edition October 10, 2015

Visit the author's website at: www.lionorfox.com

ISBN-13: 978-0692428641 Waterhorse Press LLC

Allegiant / 1

Heart Shaped Rocks / 6

The Apocalypse Rewind / 12

Zombie Bodies / 17

It Takes More Than You Got / 23

Anachronistic / 25

Mechanical Parts / 29

Things That Survived The Winter / 33

Dog vs. Wolf / 39

Petty Tyrants / 43

Dis-Missive / 51

Thresholds / 48

Building an Ark / 55

Keystones / 59

Bitte Orca / 64

Oceans Ignited / 69

Sharks in Swimming Pools / 74

Thighs like Knives / 78

Out in the Cold / 81

Reflection / 85

Crown Chakra / 93

Victor's Table / 98

What Will / 101

Allegiant

Where does my allegiance lie?
With you
Home and Country
Bloodlines
Beneath my feet

Did you notice?
The forest started to grow
How I disappeared and
My body became leaves
Shades of green and white
Scattered between objects
But not counted among them

Forward

Status update: 5/17/15

It's 3 am and I am drawing maps of the inside of my head.

Daily morals:

1.) Be a loner
2.) Don't drink caffeine after 5pm
3.) Forget the rules and your sleep
4.) Sleep is the key, but don't dream your life away

I could never write an autobiography. Who can account for what truth is?

There are so few people who know me at this stage of my life. Except you. I wake at seven, drink coffee. Check my astrology report. Scan through Facebook to see who's sick, dying, having babies, playing music, dancing, or posting something funny or inspiring. The rest of my day is more or less versions of the following routine: Rehab. Strength train. Climb the perpetual wall. Leave tired. Email. Collect data. Reach out for connection.

At the end of the day when little comes, I do as all good Americans do. I turn on the tube. I watch a movie, or some terrible reality show that makes me feel better about my life. At least I'm not the girl who couldn't hold a hammer or hunt if she was starving. I'm not saying I would win, but I would hold my own in Survivor. Forget Fear Factor, though. I wouldn't get past the part with gross eating challenges. I have enough of a complicated relationship to food.

If my waking life lacks excitement, my dream world makes up for it. I started keeping a log when my therapist suggested it five years ago, and from then on I've been recording the cinematic history of my sleep. The following is a combination of fact and fiction, a collaboration with my subconscious, i.e. the part I can't control. I hope you don't mind, but things will get a bit weird.

3/17/2015

I am directing a film under water. We are swimming fast down to the depths of the ocean, dodging falling rocks and jagged volcanic formations. It's happening quickly and fluidly with enough space for me and my crew to feel protected. In that kind of situation, you just focus on breathing. My baby is on board with the cameras traveling behind me. I am aware others thought this was too risky, but no one knew the situation like I did. I have no fear for me or my child.

Every word of this document is true.

PART ONE

Chapter One: Heart Shaped Rocks

Lionorfox self-portrait done while house-sitting in Philadelphia near the beginning of a 3 year (and counting) nomadic experiment that happened initially by accident or luck or both. Based on a photo I took in Lyon, FR at the close of my internship with Circa Contemporary Circus (AU). June / September 2013. Site: The floor at Peñasco Theater (NM).

During my last 12 hours on the ground in Lyon, France at the conclusion of an internship with Circa Contemporary Circus, I left my new friends and a company of amazing character at the train station, walking away to contemplate my new solo direction. I'd been left with the advice to rebrand my artistic vision and to address the unique circumstances of the gallery scene, all while balancing the troubled economic and artistic priorities of the States. There was no precedent for what I would be doing, no one who could guide this confrontation with the Blasted Oak and my effort to rebuild a path.

I headed on foot toward the Rhone River to contemplate my steps, and as I thought about my impending isolation I began to weep. A handsome young French man saw me crying and called out. I explained that I don't speak the language and kept walking. He ran to catch up with me and continued alongside. We spoke separate languages toward each other with some kind of confused understanding. He grabbed my hand and insisted on holding it for several blocks. I broke it off, knowing my destination was solitude.

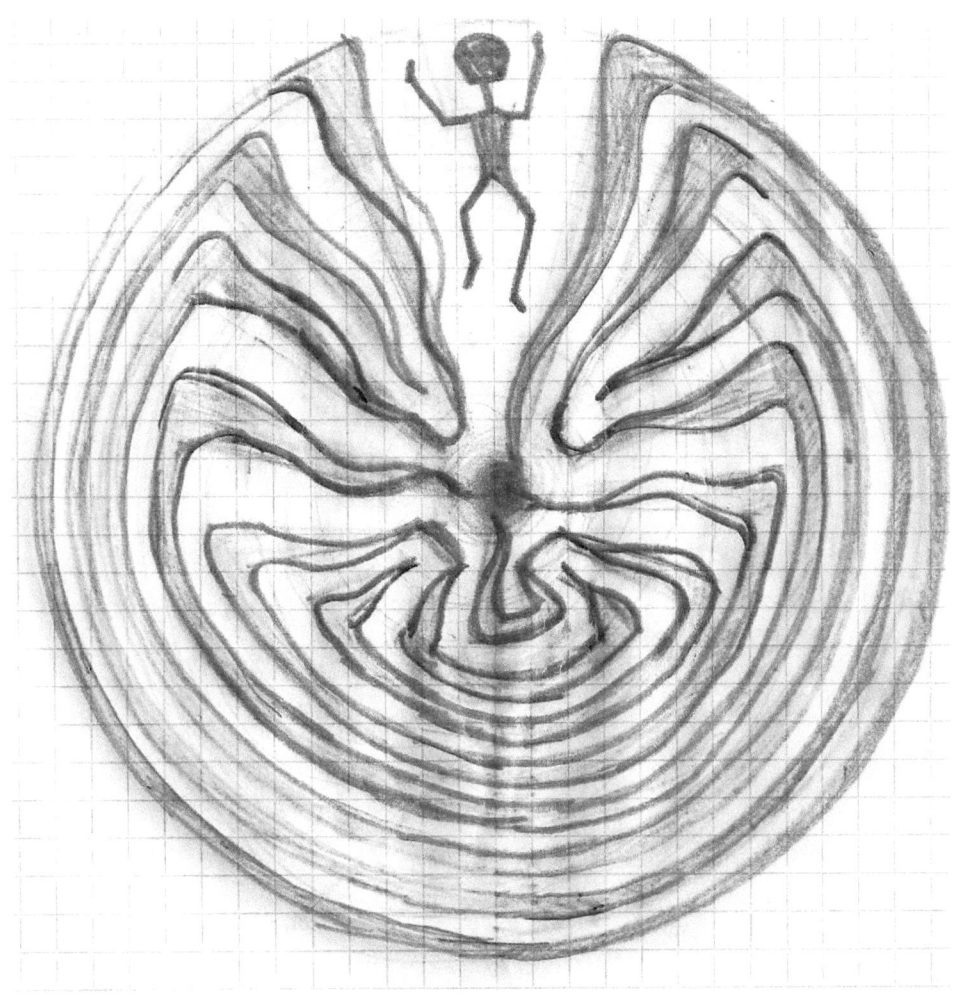

One year later, my brother Michael drew this picture of a labyrinth and gave it to me in New Mexico where I was in residence at Peñasco Theater making the solo contemporary circus show "A House for Birds". We traveled to Taos searching for hot springs, precious stones, signs and omens, and walked a labyrinth we found in front of a Unitarian Church. Days later, I went back to shoot a walking meditation and found a heart made of stones in the center of the bench. I hadn't noticed it the entire time, since I'd been filming straight down at my feet.

Center of the labyrinth in Taos, NM 2014.

Photo by Alisa Ritchie. Heron Aerial Rig made by Christina Sporrong. Taos, NM 2014.

11/7/11

I am showing guests my apartment. There are four main rooms in a square like the four chambers of a heart. I have a living room, entered first, my bedroom, two guest rooms, and a bathroom off the last. I am playing hostess when I suddenly realize I should clear out a guest room to use as a studio.

Rocks and fossils I collected and painted as a kid in Wisconsin in the 1980's and early 90's.

Chapter Two: The Apocalypse Rewind

The universe is made up of both light and dark. To deny the darkness is to assure that hidden patterns will be repeated. This is the essence of karma.

3/11/2015

I am at the gynecologist for a quick check-in and they diagnose me with HIV on my way out the door. I'm devastated and think about killing myself. I want to tell my family but can't bring myself to do it. I see my future dissolve. I will never have the love of my life or any idealistic future. I know myself, and I would never let anyone get that close.

I go to the movie theater to curl up and fall asleep across the seats. As they are filling, I move down near the front. I have a sleeping bag with me. The lights go out, the movie rolls on, and I am lulled to sleep.

~

This symbolic dream of loss came to me just after a small surgical procedure, which reconnected me to a kind of pain felt at the start of my 11-year odyssey. It shares an emotional tone with this next true story.

I was 24, and graduating with my Masters from a prestigious east-coast arts institution that I had chosen specifically to be politically challenged in my work as an artist. I tend toward intuitive and process-based creation, but felt it was important to marry logic and intellect with the esoteric. I never knew what shape my challenge would take, and I never imagined it would come in the form of a department tyrant, disability labyrinths, and an emotionally abusive relationship.

During the development of my thesis, I began to attend sessions with a fantastic therapist and mentor, Ashley King, to grab better hold of my circumstances. The two most important things she gave me were the courage to address my feelings in relationship, even when met with psychic abuse, and the advice to start a dream log, which has been a great source of inspiration over the years. Excerpted here, these journals guide my understanding and application of universal symbols, serving as a concrete record of the ghosts from my waking life.

In the midst of this reflective process, this ex and I moved when our lease ended in June 2010, hesitantly (on my part) but together, across town into an apartment we had the hardest time agreeing on, that was the "nicest" we'd lived in since moving to Philadelphia.

No part of me wanted to do this.
Nature was quick to point that out.

A few days in to the lease the apartment exploded in a plague of cockroaches. The tiny ones. They crept into the couches. The ventilation. The toaster. I quickly bought an exceptional quantity of plastic tubs to repack my life. My ex was sleeping in the bed, and I was sleeping on a yoga mat in the spare room that was supposed to be my new home-studio. Finally. I was going to have a safe space to work, since grad school had been anything but that.

HALT.
(Not so safe.)

Barry the exterminator came through every few days, drilling holes in the floor to fill with boric acid, which slowly ate away the creatures' exoskeletons. The surface of the rooms and the emotional floor were toxic.

Chapter Three: Zombie bodies

Shortly after moving myself into a first floor walk-up studio on a sketchy block in North Philadelphia, I received a three-page, single-spaced hate letter solidifying all my ex's grievances and disturbing indications of how he wanted to control me. He admitted to reading my emails and private computer documents, which he used to conduct a dramatically sociopathic personal attack. He took a false name and email, set me up for a blind date online, and stood me up. This letter was in my inbox when I got home.

The only way I can understand this change is that there was a kind-of chemical switch or circuit that flipped in him when I was in transition from Wisconsin to Philadelphia. At that point in time, I was particularly susceptible to an antisocial personality type with regards to my major health asteroid. I've often struggled with self-worth issues and the feeling that I'm a burden to those I love. Over the years it made me accept less than what I deserve, dangerously so to the point of abuse. I had three significant life lessons in this dynamic, and I tell this particular story because it's the most directly poetic.

I changed my number and passwords. By the next day, he tracked down the new number and called every day for months. I wanted, but never got a restraining order, and was told by police this would be difficult unless he showed up threatening physical violence. I heard through a mutual acquaintance he's had a kid, and I find that terrifying.

When I'd first arrived in Philly, this ex and I met a psychic named Vivienne who insisted on giving me a private tarot reading. She told me I would decide the outcome of the relationship, sending this message with an air of forewarning. Years later, a Vedic astrologer pointed out the relationship turmoil on my chart and apologized, saying he would *pass* within a few years. The idea is comforting, but I don't believe astrology can predict death so specifically. This was the first time I realized good astrologers, psychics, and therapists are all commonly smart, and do well to recognize what we need to hear.

10/14/11

I am in the car and my boyfriend collapses next to me. I pull over to the side of the road and pull him out. He's clearly dying. His heart is the problem. I split open his chest and grab it out.

There he lay, lifeless and breathless. I stop another car to ask for help and steal the driver's heart to replace the one missing in my boyfriend's chest. Somehow things improve, but it isn't enough. I have to keep swapping body parts, replacing theirs and his.

~

Several years after recording this dream, I made the connection to a Japanese folk tale discussed by Hayao Kawai in his book <u>Buddhism and the Art of Psychotherapy</u>. It seems my dream-mind adopted a similar play seven years after reading what I assume is the origin story—though perhaps this is some relic of deeply nested archetypal myth. It goes something like this:

A traveler staying overnight in a lonely hut is woken by a goblin lugging a corpse. Soon another goblin shows up, and they begin to argue over who possesses the dead body. They ask the traveler to judge and he responds that it belongs to the first. Enraged, the second goblin rips off the traveler's arm. The first goblin grabs an arm off the corpse and attaches it to replace the missing limb on the traveler's body. The second goblin responds by grabbing off the traveler's other arm. They go back and forth until the bodies are completely replaced, at which point they stop fighting and each eat half the corpse. The shocked traveler is now confused as to whether the one now alive is really him or not. He consults a monk, who tells him the "I" of a human is composed of various elements, and once he realizes what the "I" is, his suffering should disappear.

Kawai's book was my first introduction to East-West philosophical fusion. I discovered it in 2004 shortly after I had a foot of my small intestine surgically removed. If you had known me in the year prior, you would have seen me black out repeatedly and drop thirty pounds, undergoing medical mishandlings, invasive tests, and misdiagnoses. It started with a trip to the ER, where I was carried by my roommates on Halloween night after blacking out cold in the shower. I had an eight month decline that eventually led me to stop eating. At the time, I was an undergrad sophomore at UW Madison studying fashion, which I then dropped to pursue visual art.

Chapter Four: It takes more than you got

I think this dream sums up my general experience working in the Northeast.

7/19/11

I am in fictional New York and I need four batteries. I stop at a street vendor to purchase a case, but they only have packages of six. The streets are cold and grey, the vendor is overweight with matted curly hair and grubby clothes. He scolds me and says I have to purchase them all. I'm embarrassed and upset because I only want to buy what I need.

"How much are they?"
"That's not enough."

I reach into my wallet, which he takes, pulling out two twenties and several singles.

"Here we go, that's what you owe," he says, as he takes them all. I protest. I won't leave. It takes some time, but I produce a distraction, grab my money back and take off.

One of the tokens I took with me from Philadelphia on the hood of my car. Scratch mark from 2010 when the car was parked outside the cockroach apartment.

Chapter Five: Anachronistic

Shortly after the break-up and move, I began a month-long intensive yoga teacher training with Joan Hyman of YogaWorks. It saved my life. The supportive community under her skilled leadership kept my focus on growth, and I quickly started reading all the yoga philosophy I could get. When training ended, I snapped up a few practice teaching opportunities and quickly found I needed a slow build to gain confidence, experience, and enough teaching gigs to get by. Meaning I needed a JOB.

Art institutions didn't prepare me for economic reality and I found that out quickly. Luckily I'd been a craft skill junkie since childhood and spent loads of time in the dye room of my Fibers Department. I answered a two-line Craigslist ad "looking for a dyer", and ended up in one of the most interesting, anachronistic positions I could have imagined.

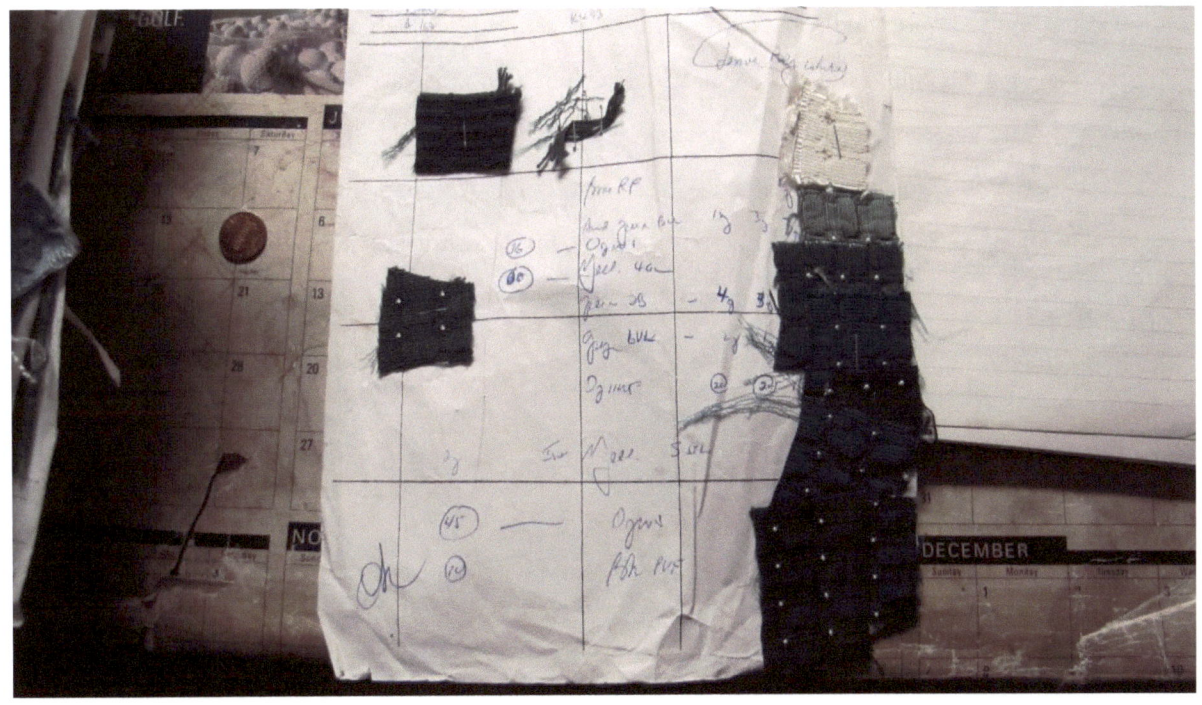

My boss Doug hired me based on the work I'd done for my thesis exhibit, much of which was made with bargain stock plastics I dyed with textile techniques to produce intricate shapes, patterns, costumes, and sculpture. The material process vaguely translates into dying vinyl, a specialty of Churchville Fabrics that carves them a unique niche in the market. Doug is a bit of a maverick and trusted me to learn on the fly. We shared a generalized life-long passion for athletics, and one can always appreciate the work ethic of a fellow jock.

Doug sent me to apprentice for six weeks in Paterson, N.J. with the fabulous Mike Petto, old school vet of the textile trade. Mike was taught when a "color eye" was still attached to a human body, at a time where skills were learned as a trade, not through University. I stayed in a hotel in Newark, drove in early, and drank tea from a foam cup. I watched him slug buckets of dye treating color like an art, layering and shading, comparing samples under different lights and nailing it with exceptional scrutiny. He saw the occasional stubborn piece, but his clients knew him as "the magician", the one who could trick nature.

The house and garage that had been converted into his workspace leaked snow through the ceiling. Mike was perpetually sloshed and colored in dye, but that was a mandatory aspect of the trade and a worthy exchange for his independence. Mike told colorful stories of the women he'd loved and of his family, though at this stage of life he flew solo. He was one of the most genuine souls I've met, a true artist, and he brought light to the darkest places.

Chapter Six: Mechanical Parts

11/17/11

I haven't remembered many dreams lately, but I have a stark image of waking up on a metal table while having surgery on my heart. My chest is cracked wide open and they are replacing it with mechanical parts.

The shop in Philly was gritty and the walls were flaking rust and covered in outdated calendars with scantily clad cheerleaders. One of my co-occupants smoked cigars indoors all day and the stench filled our shared workspace. The rest of the warehouse staff smoked cigarettes, which seemed like a lesser grievance. Despite all this I liked my job, it felt a bit like alchemy. I rarely got the same piece twice, and much of what I was dying was vintage inventory from warehouse closings scouted all over the country. My skills were constantly growing creatively in response to mystery material. The dye process allows for down-time while color develops, and I used every spare moment to write my first full-length circus script.

I was in charge of two kettles, which grew to three. Giant stainless beasts with elliptical drums and deep vats to drudge fabric through. I had a young assistant Jordan who helped load and unload fabric. He grew up in this run-down North Philly neighborhood called Frankford, which was a thriving blue collar community before the American industrial decline. One of the perks of this strange position was that my assistant would deliver weed to me at work. He was more consistent at that than he was in keeping up with his other tasks, mostly because I could never find him. The three floors of the warehouse were a dark and twisted industrial playground, and he must have found every hiding spot.

The third floor of the building, which was occasionally used to store yarn, at one point had an artist renting space. He had a business making cheesy birthday signs and props. He was also a hoarder and left in a hurry. I found lots of treasures lost in the remains of his studio.

Chapter Seven: Things that survived the winter

        My heart

        Your ego

        The flowers I planted

        Several misfired arrows

        My car

        Your distance

Hermit huts

Sheets of plastic

Animal paths

Three parallel lives

The cracks in the sidewalk

When I close my eyes

I see the black

In my nightmares

I am dying and we never met

Over the years I've been known to fall in love in an hour and get my heart broken all the time. For years I've been a moving target, which is a part of the problem I admit to, but wouldn't change. By the time I catch up with my potential darling, he has moved on in another direction.

I am not good with distance.
I am too good at distance.
It's all a matter of perspective.

Previous Page: "Modern feminine, historic man". Studio Shot, Tyler School of Art. Contemporary dress and traditional frock coat recreated from a 19th century men's pattern in dyed plastics. From my thesis exhibit "Specter Animalia". 2010.

Side-by-side of me and my grandmother.

Chapter Eight: Dog vs. Wolf

4/1/15

I am at my mother's house and we let the dog out back where he likes to wander. I look out the picture window and from afar I see him battling a wolf much larger than he is. My mother sees it but feels helpless. I charge out the back door running full speed toward the incident, rip the two apart, and Lucky and I head back inside. We are safe in captivity, quickly forgetting the intensity of the moment until CRASH! The wolf dives straight into the large picture window trying to break the glass. He charges several times with impressive strength, but is unable to break through.

Chapter Nine: Petty Tyrants

There are generational wounds I am convinced I was put on earth to contemplate. My family's bloodlines assemble an American-born Irish woman with an ex-German soldier, a former farmer who fought for Hitler, lost a brother to the war, and was an allied POW originally stationed in Massachusetts. He spent three years slammed in a French coal mine after the war was done, after which he married into a Irish family divided on both sides of the ocean, hopping a boat to join the world's victors. America was Forgiveness.

On the other side of the tree we have a kindly woman archer married to an ex-WWII POW American vet who escaped across the African desert. He represented the force of justice as an officer for the Milwaukee Police Department, but was known to have a physical temper toward his family. America was Righteous.

The impression I get is that with this post-war "shit will hit the fan" attitude, stability was nothing to trust. Each person in my family has experienced, directly or indirectly, the violent abuse of power. The rippling fear patterns are chemically bonded to our DNA.

I am always on the firing line.
Sometimes I'm the target.
Sometimes I'm holding the gun.

Above: My first gun lesson with my Uncle Don. My family has given my grandfather's revolver for protection (not pictured).

Next Page: Colleen Hooper, a Philly-based modern dancer who I regularly collaborated with during my years at Tyler.

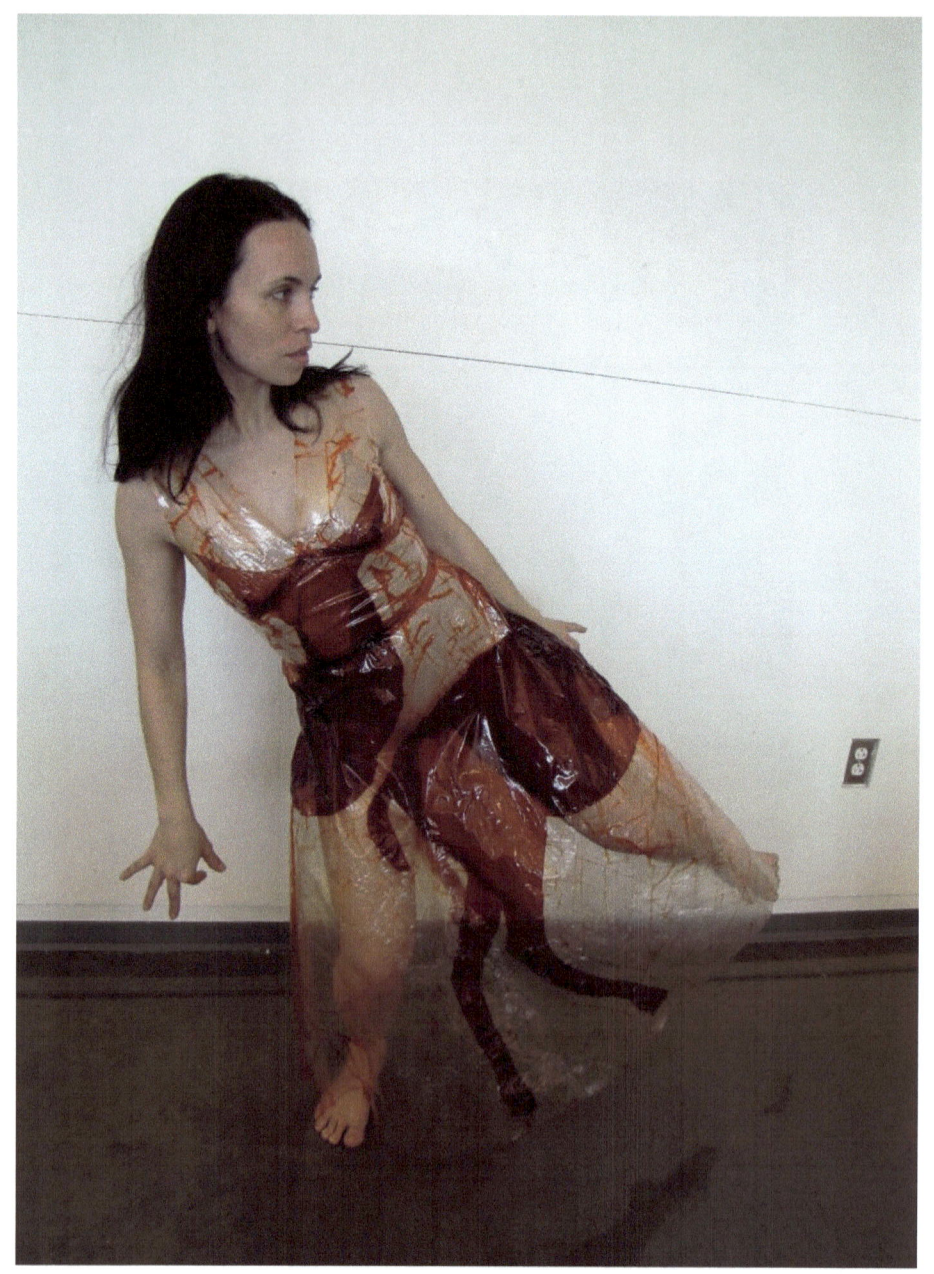

Chapter Ten: Dis-Missive

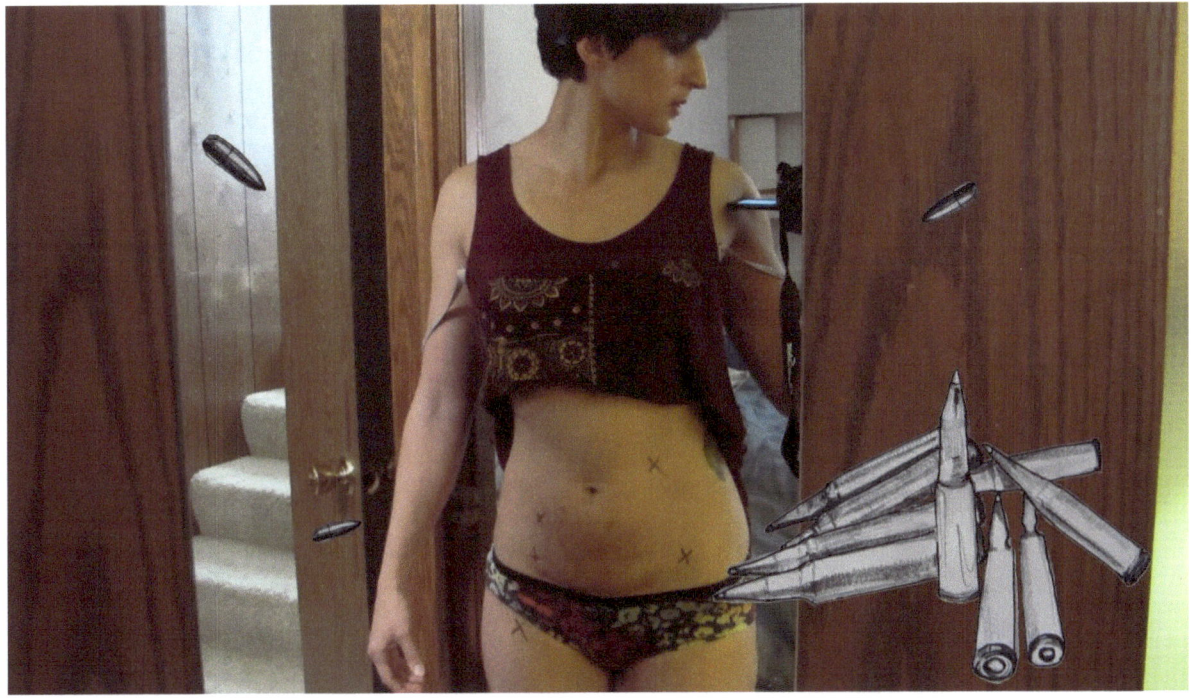

Self-portrait/ Physical Therapy Document. Here you can see my scar, and the "X's" indicate internal trigger points. 4/23/15.

10/18/11

Michael and I are attacked on our way off the beach. He has gunshot wounds in his hand and thigh, and I in the gut. We head straight to the doctor's office where we stand in line for hours. We approach the desk for help and are haughtily dismissed. I beg advice for directions to the ER. The staff chuckles, saying "We don't know". Pause. Wait. Deliberate. We set off on our way, but the ER is never found.

All this effort in vain. I stop to ask after my brother's wounds and to look at my own, only to find the marks that were once gaping and bloody are being pushed to the surface. I offer to remove his bullets with a tweezer. He becomes defensive, retracts, pauses in thought, and insists on doing it himself.

~

My three siblings and I are purging violent memories through our flesh. War on a cellular level, we are fighting ourselves. Crohns disease, my Western diagnosis, is an essential misfire of the autoimmune system, attacking my body at the core in response to food and the environment.

After major surgery and nine years of low-dose chemotherapy, I chose to work toward holistic healing through diet and lifestyle. This is a work in progress, and I live with a shadow fear of backsliding past a point of no return. The choice to drop wheat was a key factor that has made this possible, but I still have a life sentence to be challenged in receiving nourishment.

The boundary has been compromised.
ATTACK!
I am my own petty tyrant.

Chapter Eleven: Thresholds

Chapter Twelve: Building an Ark

12/1/14

I am out on the water seated on the just-surfaced remains of an old wooden ship, something of the Mayflower era that carried the first Europeans to North America. Though I lack the specifics of its history, it clearly held the power of transcontinental passage, a tool to permanently resettle. I closely study how the boards come together to support such a voyage.

We pull the frame out onto the sand and suddenly there are planes overhead. They bomb the ancient ship into oblivion. It wasn't big enough to transport the whole crew anyhow, and as all this is happening I direct the construction of a second ship. It is invisible to the planes overhead, hidden underneath a shelter covered in sand.

Message in a bottle. 2014

Embryo. 2014

PART TWO

Chapter Thirteen: Keystones

I grew up on fifteen acres of natural land in southeastern Wisconsin. My father and grandfather planted the trees which have become a thriving forest habitat for deer, coyotes, rabbits, birds of all kinds; even wolves pass through here. The location is approximately an hour's car ride from the Great Lakes and immediately on the pathway of the Monarch butterflies that alternate seasons traveling between Mexico and Canada. Every summer, my siblings and I were enchanted by the caterpillars that magically appeared to feed off the native milkweed supply in our region. We found them hidden under leaves, collected them in jars, and fed them. We watched them eat, swell, spin cocoons, turn from green to black, and emerge as butterflies leaving only a blank chrysalis behind.

 I have taken thousands of photographs of this property and walked every brambled inch. Each season on the land has its own remarkable beauty. There is a collection of photos scattered throughout this book.

There are many oak trees in our forest, and they sparked my interest after reading about their unique community structure. Trees set apart, giving each other space to grow while connecting roots in an underground vascular web. This evolution supports the recovery of an injured tree through the automatic redistribution of nutrients at times of disease or trauma. This protects a global pattern of growth that makes Oak a distinguished species not for any extreme, but for their wide-ranging survival pattern.

On this same land, we can look at the relationship between creatures of earth and air, the Monarch and the Human. Twenty years ago, our family of six couldn't collect enough peanut butter jars to house the thriving population in our yard. We gathered tables full, and left many caterpillars to weather the outdoor conditions on their own. They never "asked" for anything, but their intricate transformation was inspiring, warmed our hearts, and created our impulse to protect.

In the last few years the Monarchs have disappeared from our land. Research suggests the use of chemical pesticides devastated the Milkweed pathway between Mexico and Canada. Can you imagine traveling great distances with delicate wings while watching your food and shelter disappear beneath you? Biological evolution doesn't work that fast, but I hope that social evolution will. Humankind is the petty tyrant here, and it is a shame we give so much power to so few who hold the world's fate in their hands and seem to misjudge it.

> *The path of the righteous man is beset on all sides by the inequities of the selfish and the tyranny of evil men. Blessed is he who, in the name of charity and good will, shepherds the weak through the valley of darkness, for he is truly his brother's keeper and the finder of lost children. Ezekiel 25:17*

Above: Milkweed from my mother's land, the Monarch's sole food source. They lay eggs and spin cocoons using the leaves for protection. These plants used to be abundant in our fields, but now there are few.
Next Page: A tree mural I painted at my father's house 11/29/2013 (my birthday), commissioned by my step-mother Susie. She chose the television placement in my absence, making this an unexpectedly poignant assemblage sculpture.

Chapter Fourteen: Bitte Orca

The notion of a gift with no expectation seems basic, but is not. In certain religions Christ is its purest example, and his flesh is weighed at no less than the redemption of man. Belief in this act divides cultures worldwide, and philosophers mark it as a fundamental question of human nature. His story has an interesting relationship to pain, which here becomes ritually accepted and culturally normalized. To me it seems dangerous to think of this exchange as anything but a story, and I prefer the rebirth of the mythical Phoenix as a cult image of transformation for that reason. These layers of symbolism are deep and nuanced, and say much about our expectations and deepest wounds.

History is, of course, FULL of altruistic grey areas lost-in-translation. Another example, the term "Indian giver" is an embarrassing Americanism used to describe a transaction in which the giver demands back the gift or something of equal or greater value in return. This is thought to be a misinterpretation of the Native American barter system dating back to at least the 1700s, though the term is still applied. In European colonial tradition, trade involved money and "gifts" were given freely with nothing expected in return. Anything else was impolite.

It's interesting to compare these transactional nuances with another species in a foreign environment, here looking to the example of an Orca whale. Communities are linked socially through blood ties and through acts of kindness aimed at non-related peers. A life-saving example is when a whale is injured it is carried to the surface by mates to breathe. "Suites" of behaviors like these are evolutionary tactics that work when adopted by the whole pod in a scenario where no one "cheats". The demanding ocean environment produces this style of altruism in a species we so casually call the "Killer Whale".

As an artist trying to get by in the world, generosity, bartering, and zero-cost structures have been a necessary grey space and living experiment. I give as freely of my time and energy as I feel is possible toward individuals and communities that express their support, and in return I've learned to accept help from many directions. This includes generosities like food, couches, space, advice, skills, equipment, love, and at times money. I have not perfected the process of giving and receiving, but I always promise to be working toward improvement.

Flexible mindset allows me to develop a geographically broad and socially eclectic net. My art path required years of risky foundation building unsupported by the American formal economy. Often I've had to accept circumstances built on deep vulnerability and trust, as did my supporters. Those who know me, or got-to-know-me through this process, understand that I return my debts through relentless dedication, work produced tirelessly, and any personal resources I have available. Often this takes faith and time. Boundaries are fluid. Psychic connections are an evolving necessity.

When I have no other means to express the gratitude in my heart, I leave origami dream boxes filled with symbolic objects—feathers, keys, crystals, and artifacts I've collected from the road. The accompanying message is one of faith and support for the dreamer's intent. They are meant to hold space for the best and most true intentions we have, without limiting beliefs. I know they work, because I have seen it in my own life. Everything is energy, and energy is everything.

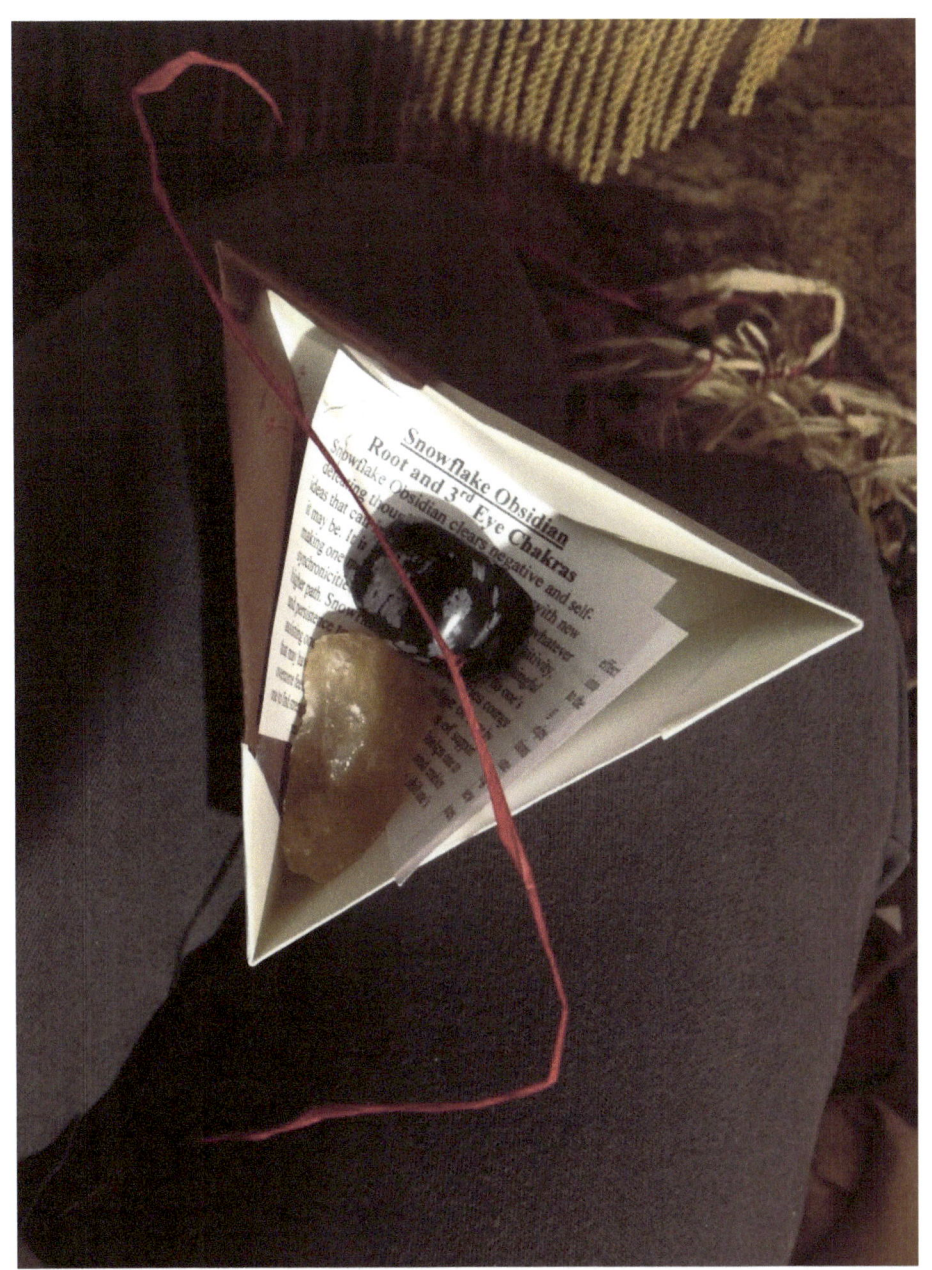

Chapter Fifteen: Oceans Ignited

The seminal dream in this series was presented to my therapist Ashley and has been included in a recording for trapeze in several variations called "Oceans Ignited". This piece was initiated following the second major BP spill in the Gulf of Mexico. Cars and oceans have been ongoing, mercurial metaphors in my life, and I imagine that holds true in reflection for many others. They are universal symbols of mobility and drive, emotions and our relationship to the body and nature, with layers of personal and cultural meaning. Black magic from the bones of our ancestors and the substance of stars fuels dreams of power beyond our innate capacities. Oil is a product of our will. It is victory.

The piece goes like this:

Next Page: A photographed run-thru of the first "Ocean's Ignited" trapeze piece. Picture by Amy Morrissey. Philadelphia School of Circus Arts. 2011.

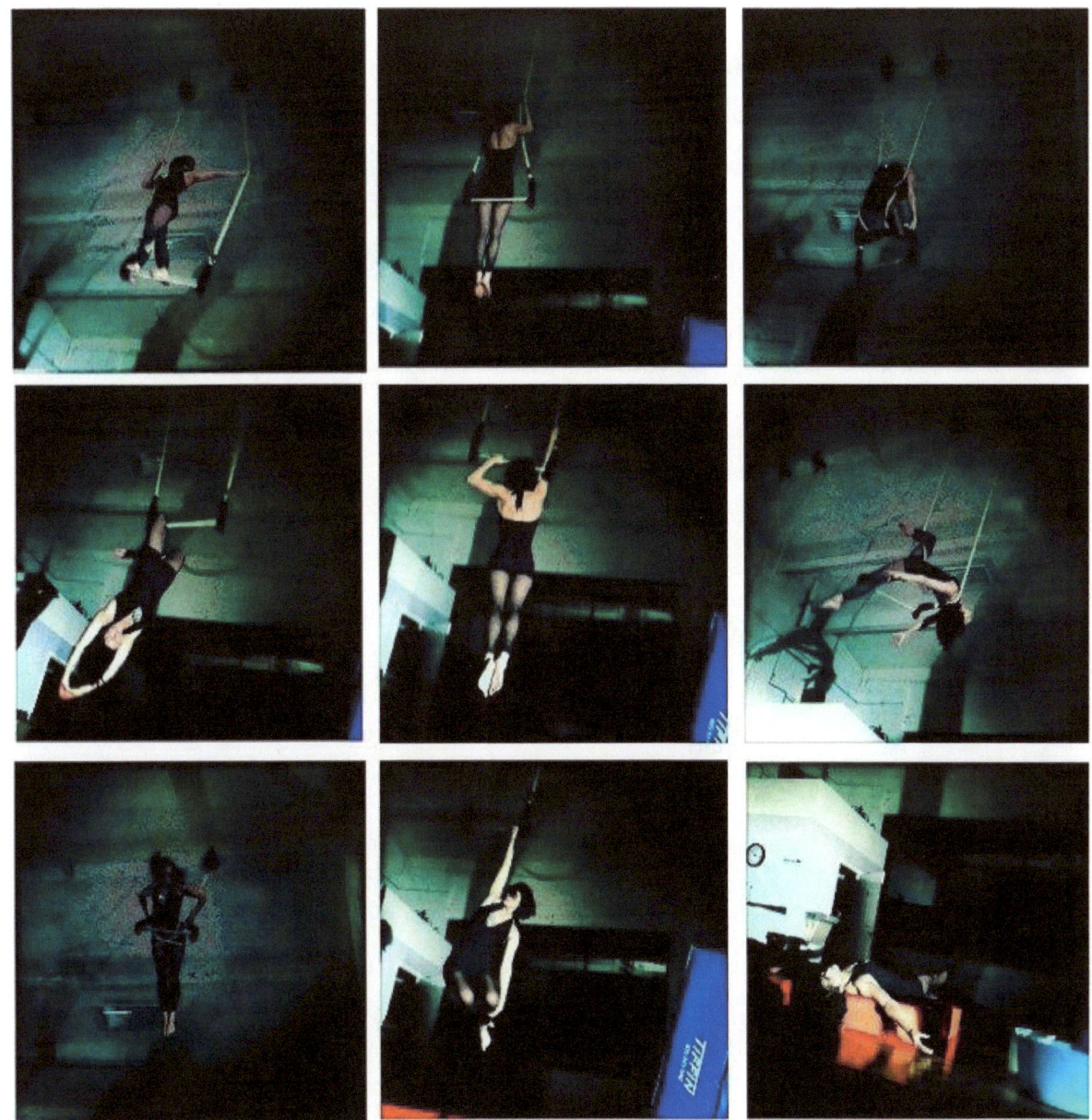

The other night I woke up in a sweat, my nightclothes twisted around my body. I couldn't remember what I'd been dreaming about, but it must've been either really good or really bad. I got up for a glass of water and caught my face in the mirror. It was me, of course. I knew that. But for a second I saw my grandmother, not as I knew her from life but from photographs. My family always told me I looked so much like her, and I always thought it was a shame that we never really spoke.

Ten minutes later I was back in bed, and what felt like ten minutes after that my alarm clock rang. They say that if you want to recall your dreams you should keep your eyes closed after waking, trying to focus in on any details you can remember. My eyes burst open and all I thought about was getting out the door. Selective amnesia.

Click of the seat belt. Security. Driving has become so routine that sometimes I forget what I'm doing and lose myself in the traffic currents. The slight discomfort of the seat belt helps to remind me of where I am. Driving, not floating.

As I drift my eyes soften and I allow myself to be carried away. I'd like to think that I'm devoting at least 50% of my attention to the road, but I'm sure that's not the case. Somehow it works out, no accidents yet. I think of it as shifting my focus to my internal third eye, letting my psychic channels guide me, but I'm not convinced that applies to mechanical extensions. Still…

Brake. Shift. Turn. Click. I have reached my destination. The Bank. Source of all tangible energy transfer. I've been operating at a deficit lately, but that's soon to change. Of course not before they try to take everything I have. I have nightmares where my car is repossessed. In my dream I find a note, a sort of love letter under my wiper blade. Starts out, well, right? A more flattering script I've never heard, and at the end it informs me, "We will be repossessing your car tomorrow". Signed Anonymous. Energy suck.

Ding, Chatter, Click. Transaction finished. There, now at least I'm safe for the week. Click. Pull. Step. Slam. Turn. Ding. Shift. Pedal. Drive. Bodies advance. Traveling at robotic paces beyond the laws of human locomotion. Bizarre how there's so much movement involved with the body so still. Gears and levers replace legs and arms. Seat-belt restrains the force of potential impact. All made possible by our alien ancestors, the bones of evolution, siphoned from wells of war.

There's no avoidance, I'm part of the cultural machine. Barely can remember how to move without oil. Bodies rust up over time. Oxidized metal forming permanent attachments. Find any life on the Gulf Coast and they've got the opposite problem. I guess that's just how it is; you're either starving or drowning for it. Black liquid gold. Seaweed cells osmose oil instead of water, turning green into black matters.

87 Days of hope lost. I drive down to the shore to help the clean-up. Straight through the night, only stopping for gas and food but not for sleep. When I arrive its past midnight, and the crew has been gone since dark. Doesn't matter, I want to see the damage for myself.

I leave my car out on the road and walk toward the beach. Once I hit sand my shoes come off so I can feel where the earth saturates. Wasteland in view. Black lacquer glaze organics into monochrome form. Involution returning shape to entangled state. Enmeshment.

They say we are born not knowing separation from the outside world. Over time our egos develop as a means to protect against displeasure, but we suffer a loss. Forever yearning for that oceanic state, that indissoluble bond with the universe, we peer through shrouds floating our heads off our bodies. Up into heaven, out into space. Embracing illusion with the conviction of saints. Freud says that love is the closest thing to experiencing boundary dissolve, but warns it's dangerously close to pathology. (*wink) Such a romantic.

Looking out for signs that I am not the only living thing on this planet. Placid ocean shows no signs of life, though there must be some and I aim to find it. Underneath the obsidian surface I imagine bodies writhing, trying to free themselves from their own oil-covered skin, unable to feel through thick layers of funereal coating.

I remove my clothes and peel off my skin down to the muscle, so I can sense the elements without obstruction. Expanding my perception, I light a match and jump in.

Oceans Ignited.

Chapter Sixteen: Sharks in Swimming Pools

2/23/14

I am watching a film in a dark stadium. The deep blue of the ocean looks painted, surreal, hypnotic. The scene unveils hunters looking for a dolphin that has a strange nose. Its adaptation allows it to swim different patterns than any other they'd seen, which makes it illusive, hard to track.

Time and space lapse. I am on a hill overlooking an old swimming pool repurposed to house aquatic life. It's filled with whales, dolphins, and sharks. I wonder whether they have enough space, and I sense that I am projected within that pool. Somehow it seems to be an improvement, though on what terms I'm not sure. I sense, but can't communicate this sentiment to others, and I am left with the phrase repeated to me by another, "People don't understand how genuinely intuitive you are".

~

Deep pressure, rocky waters and my own wounded vessel forced a unique set of adaptations in me. Deeply intuitive and outside the box, I have sought what my family lovingly calls a "Sarah-shaped crack in the world", or what I would thank Krishnamurti for, the phrase "freedom from the known". I strive to push against the boundaries of what I am told I can accomplish, and the structural constraints that keep us from a expressing a universal ethic of care.

Whale portrait / assemblage, part of the set of "A House for Birds" 2014.

Whale portrait/ shrine. "A House for Birds" 2014.

Chapter Seventeen: Thighs like Knives

5/25/2012

I am having sex with an older figure because it's "good for my career". I feel discomfort in my groin and thigh and it keeps my mind pre-occupied. The scene switches to a high-ceilinged luxury loft apartment, and when the sex ends I discover a surgical instrument lodged in my thigh. I decide to dig it out with a knife, an act that leaves a deep gouge through layers of skin and muscle. Somehow removal hurts less than embedment. The next day is a holiday and I am alone. I start to worry the wound needs stitching and call an ambulance.

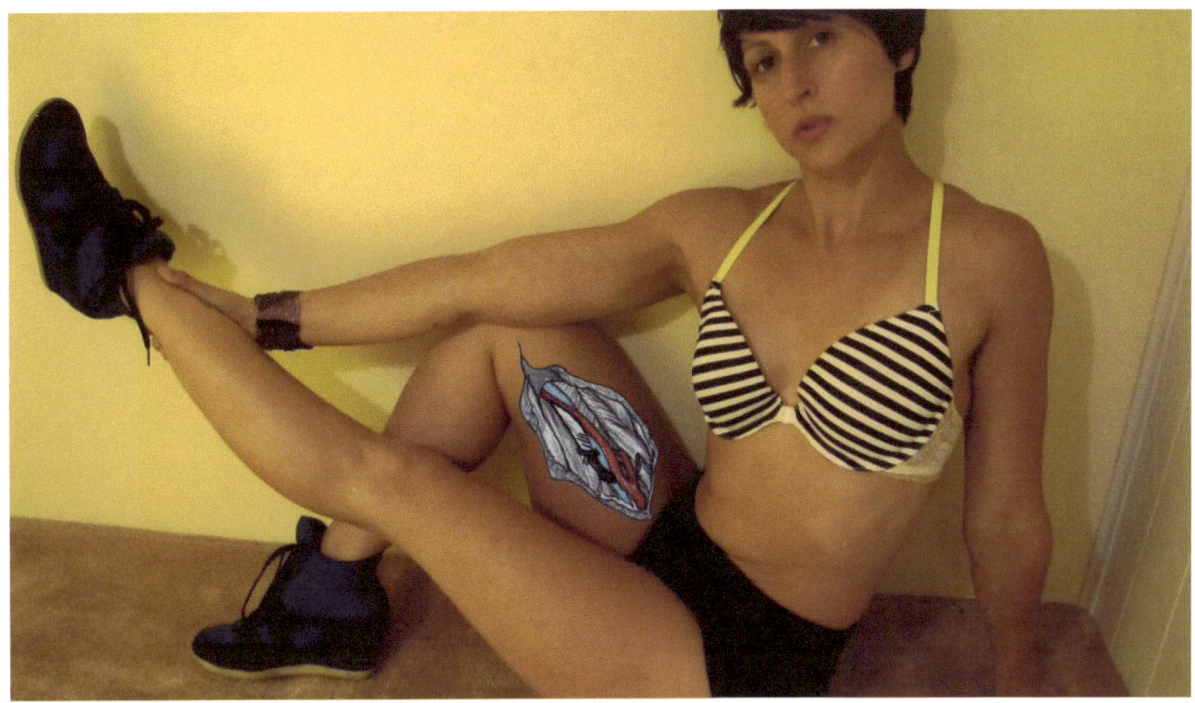

The visible scar I received in surgery cuts through layers of core creating a smile line across my pelvis. It is the same mark as a C-section, but I joke that it only gave birth to "creative babies". When I inevitably move and pull against this mark, tightness across the soft space sends freezing signals and limitations to the rest of my body. Scar tissue doesn't know how to "give. Even skilled bodyworkers and physical therapists have a difficult time dealing with it. When it's dislodged, I sense electricity shooting along a seam line where pieces of my body have been wrongly stitched.

I made the conscious choice to pursue serious athletics to keep up the discipline and physical control I needed to ensure the best quality of life for myself. It was certainly the difficult road, but I've never regretted it. The scar through my midsection serves as a barrier to use in exploring creative movement. My weakness informs my awareness as a performer and teacher, giving purpose to the amplified echoes that haunt my bones.

Chapter Eighteen: Out in the Cold

2/3/11

Dream within a dream. I am sleeping with someone attractive, but who I'm not interested in. It feels pleasant, but I sense I'm detached. I realize I need to be with someone else. Then I wake up.

I am naked in a stranger's house. It's winter in Wisconsin. I grab a towel and walk out the door into the snow, looking out over a frozen lake. I feel the snowfall on my skin, but it isn't cold. I mysteriously acquire my coat and continue walking along a windy road. I run into some friends, but they don't ask why I am naked. They are looking for a way home and I lead.

Chapter Nineteen: Reflection

At the time I am writing it's spring in Wisconsin. I'm secluded on what became my mother's land, the fifteen acres where I grew up. I've had six months of rehab, an indication that I never fully recovered from surgery and that attention and access to care was dropped to catch up with the pace of modern life. I returned to University three weeks after my operation, and I've been wheeling and dealing odd-jobs ever since. In the past ten years I've been a perpetual student, a hired dyer, seamstress, yoga teacher, un-licensed massage therapist, videographer, painter, performing aerialist, stagehand, arts writer, artist assistant, house cleaner, nude figure model, website designer, mortarer, retail associate, assembly line and food truck worker. All of these roles were adopted to support independent creation. This is my American hustle.

The biggest blessing, by force of nature not will, is that I've had time to rest and heal old wounds while living in my childhood home for the last time, as it is being sold. An example to aspire to, I believe Frida Kahlo became an artist finding light in a recovery room. So here we are again, back at the start: re-valuing the fundamentals of life and space to breathe. I hope this time through the labyrinth I will remember my lessons from the trip.

Portrait series of the light in each bedroom on the day the house closed. 7/1/2015

Chapter Twenty: Crown Chakra

Tarot reading 4/4/2015. Heart: Contra Wolf's Path. Skill Focus: The Shaman. Personal Intent: Protection. Deck is the Wildwood Tarot designed by Mark Ryan and John Matthews with art by Will Worthington.

10/9/13

I am swimming with friends in a foreign ocean. We've been living there for some time. With no warning the nation is forced to pack up and leave. I head straight to my apartment but don't know where to start. I look around and it is filled with someone else's things. I leave to find food and boxes, then realize I should head "home" to pack my belongings.

I go back to Wisconsin, to my mother's house. It is dark, but I am staring out the window and something catches my eye. It's a dove with a hole in its wing that allows light to shine through it. I grab my I-phone and try to capture it, and it bursts into flames or light or both. It's brilliant. I can't manage to call anyone over in time, so I keep snapping photos and I watch as it changes form into a girl at the back door of my mother's house. She fades and disappears.

I go to tell my family, and see that the photos I'd taken weren't stored in memory. I look back outside. The girl is gone but she left me a wooden beaded necklace with a skull on it. I take it to my mother, who hands me a complimentary piece. It's bright red and jeweled with a narrow central panel that hangs over my heart and threads into a feathered hair piece that is attached at the back of my skull. As she puts it on me, she gives it a Sanskrit name. I sense this is the key to unlocking my crown chakra. These are the skull and feather jewelry from the tarot.

I walk back through the kitchen toward the room where I witnessed the dove. Pink flowers are blooming everywhere and their leaves rapidly consume the space. My transformation is complete.

I have a tactile sense of what Frida found through her symbols, style, and adornment. To create, own, and wear art is to participate in the value structure, giving weight to works of beauty that make light and clarity of our burdens. Those of us with chronic pain are continually reminded that the material of life is precious, and that the body is made for exaltation not punishment. Through a mix of abdication and desire, a tactile sublime, we honor pride and god in human hands.

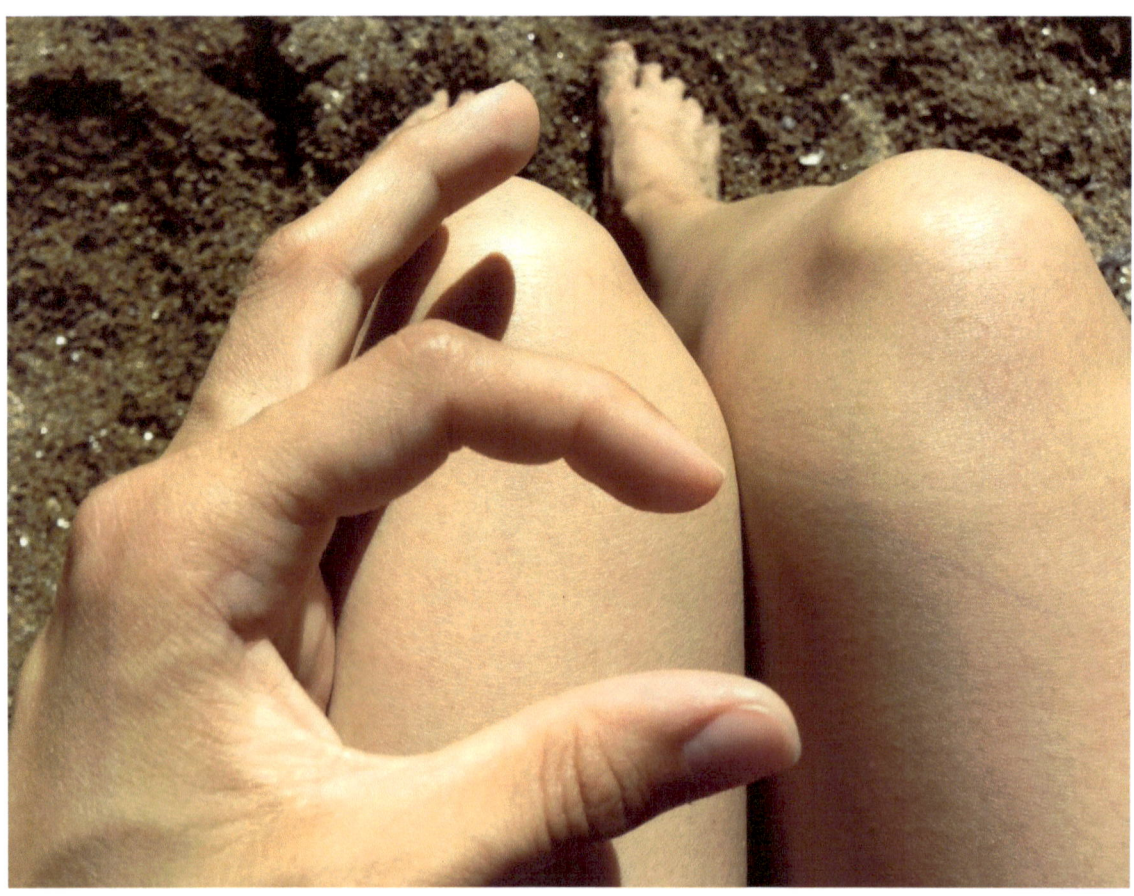

Chapter Twenty-One: Victor's Table

Heart-shaped bone. Found 4/29/15.

11/19/14

My brother Michael is soul sick. He's been tirelessly preparing pies of meat and beans and they are overflowing the kitchen, laid out on counters and the top of the fridge, mixing with cat vomit nearby. The whole scene is contaminated. He is sleeping and I am hesitant to tell him about the state of the creation he'd poured so much heart into.

Time lapse and I'm picking out a movie to watch. I choose raw footage I've been directing and haven't seen yet, strange and oceanic. Building in excitement as I realize this project will develop strongly enough to support us all. I'm alone at a computer and it's late. Everyone is sleeping. I am watching waves. On the table in front of me is a gelatinous mass growing and developing facial characteristics. It's turning into me. I see a second mass that represents my nascent boyfriend.

12/6/14

I'm greeted in an elegant restaurant by a gentlemen in a jacket and V-neck who leads me into a back room to the "Victor's Table." I sit near the wall across from the owner and asked whether he knows if there are any meals that are gluten-free. "Plenty!" he says, as he points to the menu. There are two choices. Option One: a plate full of marrow, which looks like bone-colored wood chips soaked in blood. Option Two: a "prize" deer, a sacred animal that had been difficult to hunt, whose head came still-attached to the antler. I choose the deer as the table jokes about the marrow being quite filling. I can't imagine getting through the whole plate.

1/23/15

I am in a treehouse castle-fortress situated on a cliff. The caretaker gives me a tour and shows me the ropes, leading me to a chute that drops straight down to the water below. Others join the scene, but none are as ready or willing as I to jump in. I lead, plunging to the water below.

Oak Leaves in spring. 2015.

What Will

The wind will tear, but I set to sea
The wing will break, but I fly with grace
The soil will erode, but I plant for growth
The hull will crack, but I patch and build new
The belly of the whale may turn and sink, but
If you help it breathe it will rise

I am headed for the path and my stars.

Afterward

We live in a rationalist society full of skepticism toward anything beyond our scientifically recognized senses. Ignorance is half the problem, and pop culture confuses the rest. I don't claim the term psychic, though I don't mind it either. My dream journal and tarot work provide the evidence I need to scratch the surface of another plane. This information helps me resolve physical problems, emotional nuances, and future pathways, unwinding the web of generational patterns I am part of. Contemplating key signifiers, I take control of the outcome and my destiny.

ACKNOWLEDGEMENTS

I want to thank my stars, the people who have supported me in endless waves. There are many, and it's hard to know where to start. First off, I want to thank my mother for being the most passionate supporter of my self-expression. She also saved my butt about every-other-minute through the course of this writing. I want to thank my family Deborah, Michael, Robert, Dad and Susie, Bear, Hannah, and Aunt Ruth and Uncle Mike for your miles of love and inspiring talents. Lucie Renaud, thank you for encouraging my risky Sagittarian leaps and for seeing this book from dark to light. Thank you to my dear friends Katie Miller and Lauri Granat, and to all the friends along the way who have given me love and couches. Thank you to the groups and institutions that have supported me, Peñasco Theatre, SANCA, the Give and Take Jugglers, Madison Circus Space, Circa, Anandam Dancetheatre, and A Girl in the Sky, and of course my undergrad and grad art communities, UW Madison and Tyler.

Thank you to everyone who has taken risks on my behalf. Thank you to everyone I missed on this list, everyone I've met, and everyone I have yet to meet.

With so much love,
Sarah

About the Artist

Sarah Muehlbauer is a gypsy nomad art-crusader. She stages hybrid circus narratives in collaboration with the world. You can follow her adventures online at: **www.lionorfox.com**

www.ingramcontent.com/pod-product-compliance
Lightning Source LLC
Chambersburg PA
CBHW042008150426
43195CB00002B/52